Learn the ABCs
Nn
Warren Rylands
and Eric Doty
LIGHTBOX
openlightbox.com

Go to
www.openlightbox.com
and enter this book's unique code.

ACCESS CODE

LBXV5892

Lightbox is an all-inclusive digital solution for the teaching and learning of curriculum topics in an original, groundbreaking way. Lightbox is based on National Curriculum Standards.

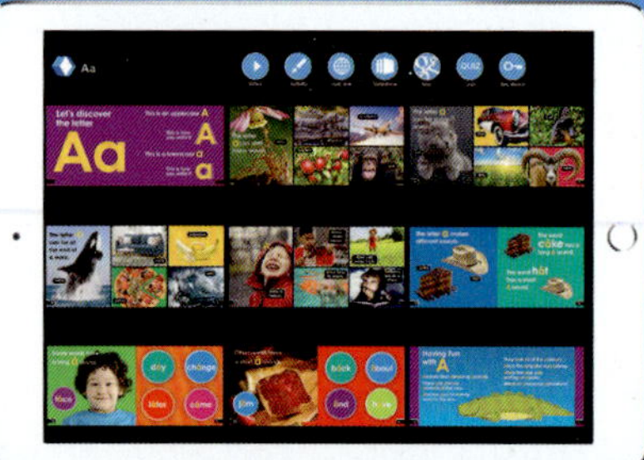

OPTIMIZED FOR

- ✓ TABLETS
- ✓ WHITEBOARDS
- ✓ COMPUTERS
- ✓ AND MUCH MORE!

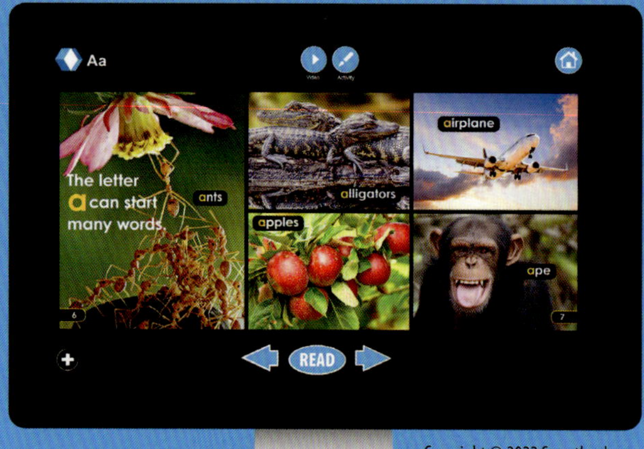

STANDARD FEATURES OF LIGHTBOX

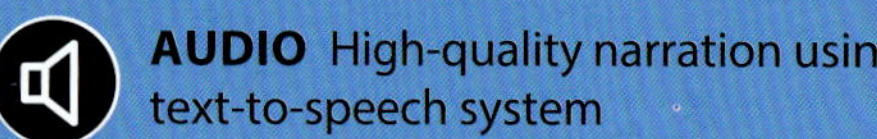

AUDIO High-quality narration using text-to-speech system

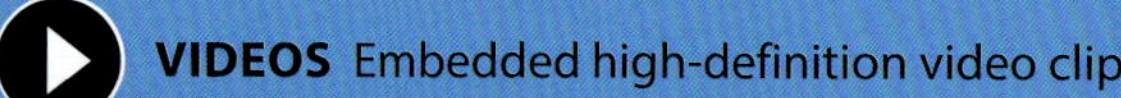

VIDEOS Embedded high-definition video clips

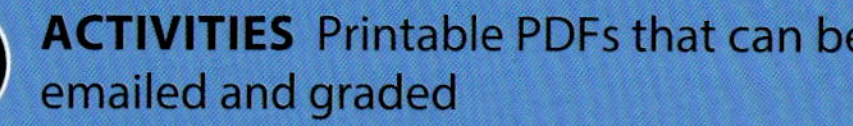

ACTIVITIES Printable PDFs that can be emailed and graded

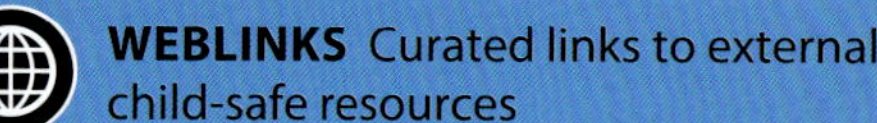

WEBLINKS Curated links to external, child-safe resources

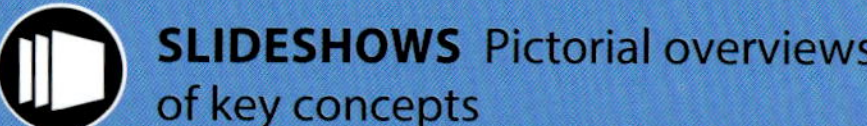

SLIDESHOWS Pictorial overviews of key concepts

INTERACTIVE MAPS Interactive maps and aerial satellite imagery

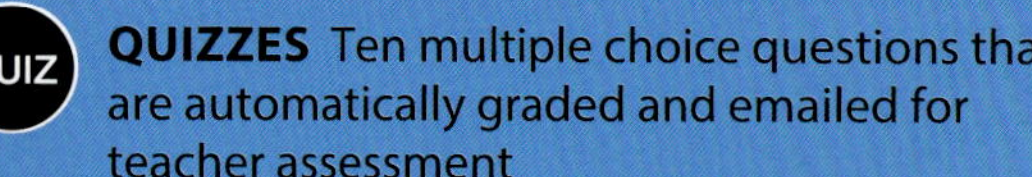

QUIZZES Ten multiple choice questions that are automatically graded and emailed for teacher assessment

KEY WORDS Matching key concepts to their definitions

VIDEOS

WEBLINKS

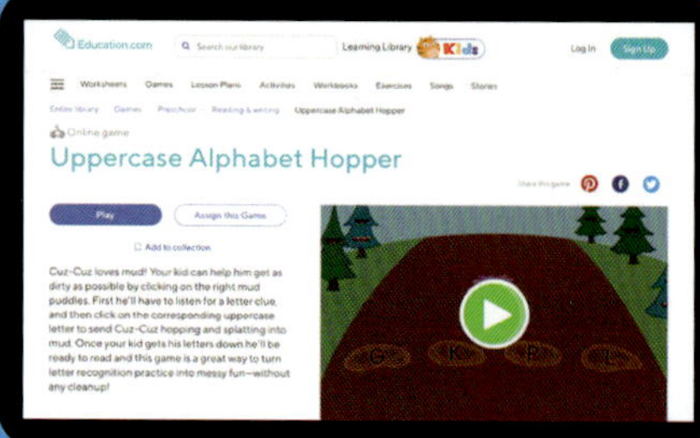

SLIDESHOWS

QUIZZES

This title is part of our Lightbox digital subscription

1-Year K–5 Subscription
ISBN 978-1-5105-5712-3

Access hundreds of Lightbox titles with our digital subscription.
Sign up for a **FREE** subscription trial at **www.openlightbox.com/trial**

CONTENTS

KEY WORDS

Research has shown that as much as 65 percent of all written material published in English is made up of 300 words. These 300 words cannot be taught using pictures or learned by sounding them out. They must be recognized by sight. This book contains 54 common sight words to help young readers improve their reading fluency and comprehension. This book also teaches young readers several important content words, such as proper nouns. These words are paired with pictures to aid in learning and improve understanding.

Page	Sight Words First Appearance
4	let, letter, the
5	a, an, how, is, it, this, write, you
6	can, many, night, start, words
8	be
10	at, end, of
12	names, takes, with
13	likes, plays, to
14	different, makes, sounds
15	in
16	man, most
17	animal, no, number, only
18	before, comes, sometimes, when
19	long, thing
20	and, another, get, into, more, not, one, there, were, would
21	too
22	has

Page	Content Words First Appearance
4	Nn
7	nail, nest, nine, nose
8	pony, rainbow
9	canoe, doughnut, pineapple
10	clown, Sun
11	brain, green, train
12	bike, Nancy, Ned, test
13	basketball, music, Nathan, Nicole, Norman
14	ring
18	king
19	song, wing
20	fun
21	Rainbow Lake, sunshine, ten
22	alphabet

Published by Smartbook Media Inc.
276 5th Avenue, Suite 704 #917
New York, NY 10001
Website: www.openlightbox.com

Library of Congress Cataloging-in-Publication Data

Names: Rylands, Warren, author. | Doty, Eric, author.
Title: Nn / Warren Rylands and Eric Doty.
Description: New York, NY : Smartbook Media Inc., [2022] | Series: Learn the ABCs | Audience: Grades K-1
Identifiers: LCCN 2020054102 (print) | LCCN 2020054103 (ebook) | ISBN 9781510557741 (library binding) | ISBN 9781510557765 (ebook other)
Subjects: LCSH: English language--Consonants--Juvenile literature. | English language--Alphabet--Juvenile literature.
Classification: LCC PE1165 .R9535 2022 (print) | LCC PE1165 (ebook) | DDC 421/.1--dc23
LC record available at https://lccn.loc.gov/2020054102
LC ebook record available at https://lccn.loc.gov/2020054103

Printed in Guangzhou, China
1 2 3 4 5 6 7 8 9 0 25 24 23 22 21

022021
110820

Art Director: Terry Paulhus **Project Coordinator:** Sara Cucini

Every reasonable effort has been made to trace ownership and to obtain permission to reprint copyright material. The publisher would be pleased to have any errors or omissions brought to its attention so that they may be corrected in subsequent printings.

The publisher acknowledges Getty Images as the primary image supplier for this title.